COSGROVE

TEXT BY JULES BAZIN
Preface Jacques de Roussan
Translator Mildred Grand
Photographs Radio-Québec
Denis Bigué
Yvon Bellemare

cordially

Stanley Cosgrove
november 1980

Stanley Cosgrove

COLLECTION

SIGNATURES

André Fortier, Editor

EDITIONS

P.O. Box 310   LaPrairie, Qué.
J5R 3Y3   (514) 659-4819

Copyright Ottawa 1980
Editions Marcel Broquet
Dépôt légal — Bibliothèque Nationale du Québec,
4e trimestre 1980.

ISBN 2-89000-030-3

Acknowledgement:

The publisher wishes to thank the Ministère des Af-
faires culturelles du Québec for its financial help in
the realization of this project.
For their collaboration:
Radio-Québec and Mr. J.P. Valentin, Galerie Art
français.

PREFACE

Gifted with great sensibility, Stanley Cosgrove is one of those painters who tirelessly pursue the same dream: that of a landscape, a portrait, a luminosity, a spirituality, which owe their vitality only to themselves. For one must speak of vitality when referring to Cosgrove. He never stops seeking the precision and the ambiency of a subject, even if this entails making variations of it from one canvas to another in the manner of a composer of music. Variations on a theme that lead us to enter into nature, whether it be a landscape or a person, always accompanied by what is gentle and poetic in it.

Cosgrove's poesy is summed up in only a few lines, since it appeals to the most *gentle* feelings, as one would have said in the eighteenth century. Accessibility of ideas, unceasing search for simple beauty, love of environment, softness of impressions... in other words, one might qualify Cosgrove a romantic, not as related to a disorderly romanticism (and there are many such), but as a supporter and an unconditional admirer of the *goodness* of things.

It is with a certain economy of means that Cosgrove tries to confide his dream to us by inscribing us in an atmosphere that, at first glance, seems to be out of fashion but which is in fact enchanting in the sense that it reveals a propensity to interior values. As if each tree, each road, each facial characteristic concealed a mystery he suggests to us but the key to which he does not wish to give us, perhaps through diffidence.

With Cosgrove there is never a question of violence, masochism or personal drama and this is the reason why he goes his own way. Nor is there any question of the esoteric or of Byzantine research. Some will say that this shows a lack of imagination, but I will say rather that it is a proof of wisdom and self-confidence. And in this last quarter of the twentieth century this is, on the whole, unusual.

Because he loves to muse over his canvas, Cosgrove is a witness of all periods and not only of his own. The human soul is rooted in the past, lives in the present and imagines the future in the same continuity or, at least, dreams that this is so, as does Cosgrove.

Jacques de Roussan

I do not believe in progress in art, progress being conceivable only in scientific and technical matter. Art only renews itself. (Stanley COSGROVE)

Stanley Cosgrove, one of the best known Quebec painters in Canada, was born in Montreal on December 23, 1911. His father, John M. Cosgrove, belonged to a family native of Newry in County Down, Northern Ireland, who had settled in Canada two generations earlier; his mother, Yvonne Morel, was a member of the La Durantaye family, whose first Canadian ancestor, Olivier, was married in Quebec City in 1670. Thus Cosgrove, from his earliest years, had the great advantage of benefitting from two cultures and of being able to express himself as well in French as in English.

There was nothing unusual about his childhood. At first, he attended a little school in St. Ann ward, near his father's place of work at the Canada Sugar Refining Company at the entrance to the Lachine Canal. Since Mrs. Cosgrove was in delicate health, the family moved to Côte des Neiges, a country district at the time, so that young Cosgrove continued his schooling at Collège Notre-Dame. The four years he spent at this institution were without incident. He felt no compulsion to draw in the margins of his schoolbooks, a habit which would have been the clear indication of artistic vocation, and it was by chance that he became a painter. His mother was very ambitious for her children — her daughter, Eileen, would become an excellent pianist; for her eldest son she dreamed of a career in commercial art, obviously without knowing that this profession had led in Canada to many artistic vocations. The industrial designer she consulted told her about the Montreal School of Fine Arts which had recently been created, and advised her to send her son to it.

Cosgrove was admitted there in the autumn of 1929. He took the compulsory general course and then spent three years in the painting class. In 1936, Cosgrove left that school and enrolled in the one at the Art Association. For two years he studied drawing with Edwin Holgate, an excellent teacher of whom he has the finest memories[1]. Much concerned with perfection, Cosgrove had just devoted almost ten years to his training.

At the time, budding artists usually spent their long vacations in personal works, completely at liberty. In 1936, thanks to the generosity of Huntley Drummond, an enlightened patron of the arts who was also president of the Bank of Montreal, Cosgrove was enabled to spend four months in the Gaspé, at the time a seldom-visited distant region. Upon his return, he naturally went to show the fruit of his work to his benefactor. Drummond bought one of his paintings and recommended him to Frank Stevens, his usual dealer, who chose some canvases and disposed of them so quickly that Cosgrove has always thought that Drummond had purchased them himself to use them as gifts for his friends.

Cosgrove used the following three summers in painting in the Charlevoix region, the chosen location of his fellow-students Jori Smith and Jean Pallardy, where he met friends, Jean-Paul Lemieux and Gordon Pfeiffer, among others. For a long time this part of the country had enjoyed great favour among artists and,

---

1. In 1939, Holgate received the commission for a mural painting for the Canadian pavilion at the Universal Exhibition in New York. This large frieze was executed at Montreal, and Cosgrove participated actively in its production. The year before, he had worked with Maurice Raymond on the decoration of St. Henry, a Montreal church, now demolished.

like them, Cosgrove brought back many canvases from there. He was with his young wife, Claire Létourneau, when he learned in the middle of September that the Quebec government had awarded him a grant of six hundred dollars to "permit him to perfect his studies in the United States" and not in Europe, where war had just broken out, cutting off his hope of going there to continue his training.

Two months after the announcement of his grant, by a fortunate coincidence Cosgrove was to hold an important exhibition at the Quebec School of Fine Arts, very close to the government building. This show comprised fifty-one paintings, one water-colour and fifteen drawings in charcoal and India ink. The earliest of these dated from 1936, and their subjects were widely varied: portraits and figures, nudes, landscapes, still lifes, genre scenes (farmers and fishermen at work), flowers. This retrospective was very well received and was fully reviewed in the newspapers of the capital. In December, Cosgrove participated in the first exhibition of the Contemporary Art Society[2].

Before following him to New York and Mexico, let us see at what point had arrived our young painter, who was still feeling his way to some extent. Art lovers and art historians have a high opinion of the works of the period before his departure, and Cosgrove is surprised at this, considering them as simple student's efforts. But all the qualities that he would soon bring to perfection are to be found here, as well as a variety of subjects whose number would lessen surprisingly later. Art historians, for their part, attach great importance to these works because they judge them worthy of taking their place in the modernist trend of the School of Paris which strongly marked the Montreal milieu in the thirties.

At the end of December 1939, Cosgrove left for New York with his wife. At first, the city made an excellent impression on him. He visited museums and galleries and saw, among others, a Picasso exhibition that contained admirable things that could help him as a painter. He spent time in antiquarian bookshops to admire old editions, went to the theatre and the movies. However, he was disappointed in the American painters; only one found merit in his eyes — John Marin[3]. This disappointment was largely compensated by the revelation bestowed on him by pictures by Gauguin, Ensor, Derain, Braque and Modigliani, which he had the opportunity of seeing, and by an exhibition of Italian art at the Museum of Modern Art. But he quickly perceived that he would not find in New York what he had come to seek and took steps without delay to obtain the authorization to go to Mexico, a country with which he had long been familiar from magazines and newspapers.

At the end of January 1940, Cosgrove left New York. Fifteen days later he was in Mexico City, with which he literally fell in love. To acclimatize himself, he travelled in the country, learning Spanish at the same time. He never tired of looking at the male and female Indians who were "magnificently beautiful with their

2. At the Frank Stevens Gallery. After his departure, Cosgrove was represented in some group exhibitions, notably at the Salon du Livre, organized in November 1940 by the Society of Canadian Writers, and at that of the Indépendants which was held successively at the Quebec Municipal Gallery and Morgan's department store in Montreal in 1941.

3. First an architect, then an individualistic painter and a brilliant aquarellist, Marin (1870-1953) applied himself particularly to depicting the plays of light and space.

black hair, their bodies of an entrancing shape and their clothing of colours impossible to describe"[4]. In April, Cosgrove enrolled at the San Carlos Academy, in the drawing class of the director, Manuel Rodriguez Lozano. The latter, who had a horror of charcoal, made his new pupil understand that drawing is not necessarily charcoal on a piece of paper. Cosgrove immediately began to draw in pencil, without shadow. He realized that with this method one must first look and observe, and soon knew that it was easier for him to perceive the essential lines of what he saw in the street. Cosgrove went to the Academy every morning, drew a great deal, refrained from painting, and in the evening took courses in wood-engraving and in lithography. Two months later he set to work seriously for the exhibition which would mark his return to Canada. After a stay of a year and a half in Mexico, he already possessed sixty pictures and some two hundred drawings.

It was then, in 1942, that he made the acquaintance of José Clemente Orozco. Upon seeing Cosgrove's drawing the master, who had just received the commission for a large fresco[5], offered to teach him his craft. By his diligence Cosgrove immediately made himself indispensable[6]. His chief work consisted of preparing the section of wall — from five to fifteen metres according to the complexity of the subject — that Orozco painted at each session, after having mixed his colours himself. The master put the finishing touches to the work with big paint-brushes, without preliminary drawings or studies, being satisfied with a pencil sketch on tracing-paper, a way of working that gave his works their great richness of tone. When Cosgrove left him in May 1943, after eight months of close collaboration, he had acquired the full mastery of this difficult technique.

Orozco had very firm socio-economic ideas and used to become really loquacious on these subjects in spite of his habitual taciturnity. For him art, of which the human being is the mainspring and the end, must, as in the Middle Ages, teach the people and awaken their collective awareness. Therefore, the artist should guard himself as from the plague against the theory of art for the sake of art. Of all these grand ideas Cosgrove retained only two things: humility and respect for the public.

A certain influence of Orozco's vigorous style, nevertheless, makes itself felt in some of the works of this period. This is particularly to be seen in religious compositions and in drawings with powerful shadows, as well as in some pictures in dull tones where among the blacks and the blues deep reds and soft rich whites sing in muted fashion. Unquestionably too, a part of his subsequent work arises from the technique of fresco[7].

---

4. From a letter of April 7, 1940 to the author.
5. This fresco, on the theme of the Apocalypse according to Saint John, was painted in the chapel of the Jesús de Nazaret Hospital, founded by Cortez in 1525.
6. This is what his work consisted of: smoothing the coat; establishing guide marks from Orozco's sketches; applying a first coat of paint like a wash; polishing the surface after the drying with a spatula in order to bring out the residual dampness.
7. On this subject, I am reminded of a topical anecdote: Fernand Léger had been invited in 1945 to be on the jury of the Artistic Competition of the Province. Upon seeing Cosgrove's entry, he exclaimed, obviously to belittle it, "What on earth is this Romanesque painting?"

Underwoods

Shortly before his departure from Mexico in the middle of October 1944, Cosgrove was invited to exhibit at the Benjamin Franklin Library. To respond to this mark of esteem, he presented thirty-eight of the paintings and drawings of his Mexican production. This exhibition was very well received by a select public and the critics judged that Cosgrove had become one of the most original painters not only of Canada but even of Mexico[8]. Some time before, he had learned that Maillard was thinking of giving him his painting class. The idea of teaching and losing a good deal of his freedom as a painter did not appeal greatly to Cosgrove, but he saw in it the opportunity of acquiring useful experience and the means of supporting his family.

Upon his return, Cosgrove soon realized that the artistic situation was very different from the one that had prevailed at the time of his departure. At Toronto, the thirties had been dominated by the Canadian Group of Painters, successors to the Group of Seven. Some of its adherents were Montrealers, notably certain of the former members of the Beaver Hall Hill Group who, in the majority, had been taught by William Brymner at the Art Association School and who, like their master, had studied in Paris. At Montreal, in the process of becoming internationalized, the situation was much more complex. Most of the known painters were of British origin but, on account of their training, they entertained no prejudice against the French culture. On the contrary[9].

This was specially the case of John Lyman, who had married a French-Canadian and had spent half his life in Paris, where he had known Morrice and Matisse. A man of great culture, he returned to Montreal in 1931 and contributed to a large extent to the evolution of artistic ideas. In 1937, with several artists he formed the Eastern Group, whose aesthetics clearly arose from the School of Paris[10]. The following year, he founded the Contemporary Art Society. Comprising artists and lay members, its main objective was the union of all those who wished to shake off the domination of academic art and for some years it played a leading rôle. Lyman was the first president and Borduas the vice-president. This association would disappear in 1948 during dissensions provoked by the automatists, students of Borduas at the École du Meuble. Furthermore, we must emphasize the infinitely less noisy presence of the former pupils of the Fine Arts Schools and the Art Association who were feeling their way and, for the most part, were taking the path of teaching.

Pellan had come back to Canada in 1940 after spending almost fifteen years in Paris and being actively involved in all the avant-garde movements. Exhibitions at Quebec and Montreal, genuine retrospectives, had made him favourably known in all milieus. In 1943 he was imposed on Maillard as a professor of painting, which provoked a real quarrel two years later between the old and the modern. The newspapers took hold of the affair and noisy demonstrations followed, which led the School's director to retire. Meanwhile, the course in decorative

8. He returned twice to Mexico: in 1947 with journalist Paul Bouchard and in 1958 with his second wife, but he brought back neither paintings nor drawings from these trips.
9. Robert Ayre, Montreal correspondant of *Maritime Art* magazine of Halifax and later co-director of *Canadian Art* of Ottawa, contributed greatly to making Montreal art known throughout the country. Cosgrove owes him much in this respect.
10. Their last exhibition took place in 1950.

Nude Study, 1959

composition was given to Cosgrove. The next year, on the request of some of the students, they created a second painting class for him, which caused between Pellan and Cosgrove a potentially fruitful rivalry that the quarrelsome atmosphere prevailing then at the School unfortunately caused to degenerate into veiled hostility. In 1948, a course in fresco was added to Cosgrove's professorial duties.

In 1953, Cosgrove was entitled to sabbatical leave. He obtained a travel grant from the federal government and for a year, with Goodridge Roberts, who had also received a bursary, he visited several of the museums of France and Spain; then he went to the Côte d'Azur to paint landscapes. He brought back some thirty canvases.

Cosgrove taught until 1958. For about ten years, different movements — Automatism, Prisme d'yeux, Sagittaires, Montreal Association of Non-Figurative Artists, Plasticism — divided the Montreal scene and created an atmosphere more or less conducive to the peaceful exercise of art.

Cosgrove, who is of well-balanced and serious mind, and had known for a long time the path he wished to follow, took great care to avoid being involved in struggles that seemed fruitless to him. To find peace, he decided to abandon teaching and henceforth, to devote himself only to painting.

Under the circumstances, this meant, at the most, a calculated risk. Indeed, his presence in many museums, his participation in Canadian and foreign biennales, the numerous references to his work in books and art magazines, the sustained interest of connoisseurs and galleries had made him favourably known in the whole country, and it is no exaggeration to say that he was, until these recent years, one of the rare Canadian artists to live exclusively from his painting.

To make sure of his tranquillity, Cosgrove left Montreal for La Tuque, where he lived for the five years from 1962 to 1967[11]. Then he spent three years at Coaticook, the native city of his second wife. In 1970, he bought and restored with very special care and perfect taste a large Victorian house at Hudson which dates from the middle of the last century. A lover of Old Montreal, he also successively had pied-à-terre on Bonsecours and De Brésoles streets.

Very early, Cosgrove became aware of his capacities and the goal he wished to reach. Since then, he has continued on his way and nothing can swerve him from his path. Originality for itself interests him not the slightest: his originality is to express himself according to the road he has chosen without troubling himself with the theories that incessantly agitate an art world in pursuit of novelty at all costs. His manner, so special that it is impossible to imitate or even copy it, is characterized by the moderation and balance of the composition, a drawing that depicts the form with one single stroke and tone relationships of an extreme delicacy. In short, it is a painting for a connoisseur. His works do not allow themselves to be understood at first glance: to appreciate them at their proper value one must look at them a long time, one by one, because their real meaning and their poetic value are hidden under an apparent facility, fruit of half a century of constant reflection.

It is useless to linger at seeking in Cosgrove's works

---

11. During his stay at La Tuque he had built at Lake Wayagamack a cottage and a studio that he still owns.

Nude Study, 1959

the influences that might have marked him, or examining them to discover some characteristic of Matisse or shade of Derain or Morandi. Cosgrove is a great reader and observer, so that it is not impossible to find sometimes in his works some unconscious reminder of a painting or a drawing he saw.

We can group Cosgrove's works under four principal themes: landscape, figure, head and still life. During a recent televised programme, he revealed that at the moment he sets to work he is seized by fright — this is the case with many artists — and that, as with the antique sculptor La Fontaine spoke of, he does not know whether the work he is beginning will be landscape, figure or still life. This statement might seem hard to believe, but it is true. In fact, any theme, or almost any one, could serve as pretext for the exercise of his art.

Of all of Cosgrove's paintings, it is the landscapes that have been the least understood. To a critic who recently brought the conversation around to this subject, the artist pleasantly answered that he does not paint trees but verticals and horizontals on a forest background. A way to inform that trees are only a pretext to express his feelings, that they are uniquely coloured harmonies.

Canadian landscape-painters long sought their inspiration in Europe, chiefly in Holland and France. To the representation of nature domesticated by man succeeded, with the Group of Seven, that of vast northern spaces battered by the wind, untamed mountains or barely-settled lands. The influence of the School of Paris, in its turn, put an end to this too-exclusive domination. In the thirties and forties many painters, Goodridge Roberts and De Tonnancour among others, participated in the return of classic landscape, to which they added a clearly local connotation but, generally, without human presence.

It is in landscape that we can best study the evolution of Cosgrove's style. In his first works, as well as in those he painted in Mexico, there are very often figures as, for instance, in *Le Buggy*, 1936. They would disappear during the fifties from his landscapes which, at the same time, would refer less and less to a particular place. It was no longer a matter of beauty of imitation, of representation, as defined by Diderot, the conformity of the image with the original, nor of the painting with a decorative purpose; the image counted very little in itself, and no first reading could encompass the richness of his work.

During the forties and fifties Cosgrove painted a series of large landscapes which are absolutely admirable. As at his beginnings, the form of the trees is drawn, although sometimes it is hardly sketched. Some of these pictures even have a vague surrealistic appearance, without counting those of the pink period which are very daring. Doubtless inspired by his sojourn at La Tuque, Cosgrove painted pictures whose principal element is snow (it is true that it sometimes appears in some large earlier pictures). When I see some of these snow landscapes again with my mind's eye, particularly one of those in his exhibition at Galerie Kastel in 1976, I cannot refrain from thinking of one of Morrice's masterpieces, *The Ferry, Quebec*, in the National Museum in Ottawa.

Cosgrove, who does not fear paradox, declares that his landscapes seem to him more and more beautiful, richer and richer in tone and treatment. Some of the recent ones, in which blacks and browns predominate and where volume is scarcely suggested, almost prove him right, since his plastic evolution has consisted of moving away from graphism in order to increase the power of suggestion of his art.

The Buggy, 1936

Sketches

15

The same qualities are found in the figures and the heads. Cosgrove is very gifted in portraiture but he never wanted to restrict himself to this because he would not like anyone to interfere in his work and squabble over the resemblance. I know only his portraits of his mother, his sister Eileen, his brother Leo, his self-portrait, as well as those of Claire Létourneau and Ann Dodds, his second wife [12]. Even if these are not *finished* portraits, I cannot help considering, whatever Cosgrove feels, that many heads that he painted or drew throughout his career, without the persons who inspired him posing, are not very far removed from the art of *portraiture* as the Clouets practised it. However, Cosgrove is right, since we generally find in his *imagined* heads and figures the same pictorial qualities, the same research of tone on tone as in his landscapes. And these women, as perceptive critics have noticed, often have a sort of interior look that produces a strong impression of sensuality, while the heads, rather small in relationship to the rest of the body, acquire great elegance from it. To the figures and the heads are added some large nudes which, in spite of the economy of means, nonetheless give an extraordinary sensation of plastic fullness. In the domain of the nude, Cosgrove, very sensitive to feminine beauty, has triumphed since his beginnings, thanks, at least in part, to the training received in schools. In this production abound, in all sizes, exquisite works where one wonders if it is colour or drawing that takes precedence.

Finally, among Cosgrove's work are many still lifes. "At the beginning," he says modestly, "I was trying to amaze myself." Perhaps, but he also amazed others, because art lovers still contend for these. And rightly, too, because most of these still lifes are completely successful and give the viewer a true enchantment through the moderation and balance of the composition, their richness despite the simplicity of the colour, their masterly arrangement, their restrained field, voluntarily limited.

Cosgrove has painted only a few flower pictures, and this is unfortunate since those he has produced are very beautiful. But, there again, they are not real flowers but coloured harmonies that have no relationship with nature, whether through colour or through drawing. His reserve concerning this theme doubtless arises from the fact that flowers lend themselves too easily to decorative play and do not offer Cosgrove the opportunity to make use of his habitual tonal research.

A few remarks on Cosgrove's pictorial technique[13]. In all his subjects, just as in landscape, form is blurred and, although always underlying, seems almost to disappear. The pictorial coat, despite the successive layers of the tones placed one upon the other, always remains thin and sometimes, especially in the still lifes, allows the canvas to show through.

It was said of Monet that he was not a colourist but a painter of tonal values who sought to depict the imperceptible only by means of colour. It is no exaggeration to state that this is also true of Cosgrove, in whose work the relationships of tones predominate. The whole can at first appear gray and dull, but the viewer is soon won over by the delicacy of colouring, displayed by unobtrusive but cleverly placed accents.

Cosgrove's work is not limited to painting and drawing. Before having access to pure art that was offered

---

12. Offset reproductions of this beautiful half-length portrait, drawing which bears the date 1957, were offered as a premium by *Canadian Art* magazine, and certainly contributed to make Cosgrove favourably known all over the country.

13. As support for his paintings he uses canvas, composition board or canvas board.

in the painting class, Cosgrove had taken, like all the students at the Fine Arts School, and later, given the course in decorative composition. Therefore, we must not be surprised that he took part in a venture in silk-screen impressions on fabric. Sponsored under the name of Canadart by Morgan's department store, this project did not achieve the anticipated success and was soon abandoned[14].

In order for a wider public to have access to his art, Cosgrove authorized some of his works to be reproduced in many copies. The earliest is a serigraph from the *Nature morte au vase bleu* published in seventy copies by Peter Freygood. Next, came *Portrait d'Ann Dodds*, offset-printed for *Canadian Art* magazine. In 1978, Michel Bourguignon published, in one hundred twenty-five copies, a series of seven serigraphs. Last year, Galerie l'Art Français printed, in one hundred copies, three serigraphs, two etchings and an aquatint. Finally, Cosgrove recently provided six drawings, one being in colour, destined to illustrate *Choix de poèmes érotiques du 16ᵉ au 19ᵉ siècle* that the same gallery has just published in one hundred copies.

Aside from all the more or less fleeting movements that occupy the Canadian scene, Cosgrove, knowing that nothing ages more swiftly than novelty, continues to paint as though he lived in a world apart. Seeking his inspiration within himself, he is a romantic artist in the true sense of the word, a poet of form and colour.

Jules Bazin

14. The cover of issue 60 of *Canadian Art* magazine reproduced in colour a composition by Cosgrove. Borduas, La Palme, Raymond and Jeanne Rhéaume also participated in this venture.

Listening to Music, 1951

PORTRAIT OF THE ARTIST'S MOTHER,   C.1936,   Oil,   45 x 37 cm
Private Collection

LA MALBAIE BAY AT BARACHOIS,   1936,   Oil,   35 x 42 cm
Artist's Collection

MEXICAN WOMAN,   1943,   38 x 33 cm
Mrs. and Mr. J.P. Valentin

NEAR CUERNAVACA,   C.1943,   Oil,   45,5 x 61 cm
Private Collection

BROWN TREES,   1943,   Oil on canvas,   40,5 x 51 cm
Mr. Claude Laberge Collection

BOUQUET, 1943, Oil, 109,5 x 83,5 cm
Private Collection

YOUNG WOMAN THINKING,   1947,   Oil on paper,   61 x 48 cm
Galerie l'Art français Collection

"THE DRAPÉ", **1948,** Oil, 71 x 91,5 cm
Private Collection

UNDERWOODS IN BROWN,   1954,
Oil on canvas,   25,5 x 30,5 cm
Mrs. and Mr. J.P. Valentin Collection

END OF WINTER,   1950,
Oil,   91,5 x 122 cm
Galerie l'Art français Collection

UNDERWOODS, 1955, Oil, 30,5 x 25,5 cm
Galerie l'Art français Collection

CROSS PATH,   1950,   Oil on cardboard,   35,5 x 45,5 cm
Galerie l'Art français Collection

STILL LIFE,   1950,   Oil,   24 x 29 cm
Private Collection

UNDERWOODS IN AUTUMN, 1950,
Oil, 71 x 81 cm
Private Collection

LANDSCAPE, C.1950,
Oil, 63,5 x 81 cm
Private Collection

DREAM,   1952,   Oil,   35,5 x 30,5 cm
Private Collection

BACK VIEW OF A NUDE STUDY,   1952,   Oil,   91,5 x 61 cm
Private Collection

STILL LIFE WITH RED JUG,   C.1952,   Oil,   51 x 61 cm
Private Collection

STILL LIFE WITH THE WHITE FRUIT-BOWL,   1952,   Oil,   25,5 x 30,5 cm
Private Collection

LA TUQUE, 1952, Oil on canvas, 56 x 76 cm
Mrs. Jacqueline Brien Collection

HALF-LENGTH PORTRAIT OF A YOUNG GIRL,   C.1952,   Oil on paper,   43 x 35,5 cm
Private Collection

STILL LIFE WITH ORANGES,   C.1952,   Oil,   40,5 x 51 cm
Private Collection

STUDY FOR THE "PRESENTATION OF THE BLESSED VIRGIN MARY AT THE TEMPLE",
1953, Oil, 43 x 35,5 cm
Private Collection

ORANGE AND BLUE JUG, 1953, Oil on masonite, 53,5 x 66 cm
Mr. Claude Laberge Collection

WHITE JUG AND LEMON,   1953,   Oil,   50 x 59 cm
Art Gallery of Vancouver Collection

41

QUARRY IN PROVENCE, FRANCE,   1954,   Oil,   63,5 x 91,5 cm
Private Collection

TREES AT **OKA**,   1957,   Oil,   40,5 x 71 cm
Club Saint-**Denis** Collection

PORTRAIT OF ANN,   1957,   Pencil,   40 x 53 cm
Private Collection

THE THREE PEARS,   1957,   Oil,   51 x 61 cm
Private Collection

HALF-LENGTH PORTRAIT OF A YOUNG WOMAN, 1959
Oil on paper, 30,5 x 33 cm
Private Collection

NUDE SITTING, 1959,
Drawing, 33 x 25,5 cm
Private Collection

MOTHERHOOD, 1960, Pastel, 66 x 47 cm
Private Collection

FLOWERS, 1962, Oil, 30,5 x 23 cm
Mrs. and Mr. Gilles Hébert Collection

ANN, 1960,
Oil, 40,5 x 51 cm
Private Collection

HEAD OF A YOUNG GIRL, C.1962,
Pastel, 43 x 35,5 cm
Galerie l'Art français Collection

BOUQUET, C.1964, Oil, 30,5 x 25,5 cm
Galerie l'Art français Collection

FIRE-SWEPT, 1964, Oil on panel, 35,5 x 45,5 cm
Private Collection

FOREST IN NOVEMBER,   1964,   Oil,   63,5 x 81,5 cm
Private Collection

TREES, 1965, Oil, 81 x 63,5 cm
Private Collection

53

STILL LIFE,   1965,   Oil,   25,5 x 30,5 cm
Private Collection

54

ST. MAURICE RIVER, EARLY WINTER,   1966,   Oil,   63,5 x 81 cm
Private Collection

AUTUMN, 1966, Oil on canvas, 51 x 61 cm
Mrs. Louise-Marie Laberge Collection

THE LAKE, 1966, Oil, 63,5 x 84 cm
Private Collection

BOUQUET OF TREES,   1967,   Oil,   63,5 x 81 cm
Private Collection

THE ROAD,   1967,   Oil,   51 x 61 cm
Galerie l'Art français Collection

APPLE AND PEAR, 1967,
Drawing, 23 x 25,5 cm
Private Collection

STILL LIFE WITH WHITE BOWL, 1967,
Oil, 30,5 x 40,5 cm
Galerie l'Art français Collection

60

NUDE LYING,   1967,
Drawing with Pastel,   33 x 43 cm
Private Collection

HEAD OF A YOUNG WOMAN,   1968,
Oil,   30,5 x 25,5 cm
Mr. W. Drummond Collection

LANDSCAPE, 1969, Oil, 51 x 61 cm
Private Collection

STILL LIFE WITH WHITE JUG,   C.1969,   Oil,   25,5 x 30,5 cm
Private Collection

UNDERWOODS, 1969, Oil, 28 x 32 cm
Private Collection

UNDERWOODS, C.1970, Oil, 51 x 61 cm
Private Collection

STILL LIFE,   1970,   Oil,   30,5 x 40,5 cm
Galerie l'Art français Collection

SHADED ROAD,   1971,   Oil,   25,5 x 30,5 cm
Private Collection

WOOD EDGE, 1971, Oil, 61 x 51 cm
Private Collection

HEAD OF A YOUNG WOMAN,   1971,   Oil,   30,5 x 25,5 cm
Private Collection

ROSES, 1971, Oil, 30,5 x 40,5 cm
Mrs. Monique Gagnon Collection

ROAD IN WINTER,   1972,   Oil,   25,5 x 30,5 cm
Artist's Collection

LANDSCAPE IN GREEN,   1972,   Oil,   51 x 61 cm
Private Collection

NATURE MORTE AU VERRE BLEU,   1972,   Huile,   20,5 x 40,5 cm
Collection privée

PORTRAIT DE GENEVIÈVE, 1972, Huile, 30,5 x 25,5 cm
Collection privée

ARBRE BRUN,   1972,   Huile,   61 x 51 cm
Collection privée

L'HIVER AU QUÉBEC, 1973, Huile sur carton, 30,5 x 40,5 cm
Collection privée

ARBRES, 1973, Huile, 30,5 x 40,5 cm
Collection Mme et M. Gilles Lesage

DEUX NUS COUCHÉS, 1974, Pastel, 38 x 46 cm
Collection privée

BOUQUET D'ARBRES, 1974, Pastel, 35,5 x 28 cm
Collection privée

NATURE MORTE AUX RAISINS,   1975,   Huile,   30,5 x 40,5 cm
Collection privée

HEAD OF A YOUNG GIRL,   1975,   Sanguine,   23 x 28 cm
Private Collection

SUMMER GLEAM,   1976,   Oil,   51 x 40,5 cm
Artist's Collection

SUMMER LANDSCAPE, 1976, Oil, 51 x 61 cm
Private Collection

UNDERWOODS, 1976, Oil, 40,5 x 30,5 cm
Galerie l'Art français Collection

TO THE RIVER,   1976,   Oil,   61 x 51 cm
Private Collection

85

BLUE SKY,   1976,   Oil on canvas,   51 x 61 cm
Private Collection

AWAITING,   1978,   Drawing,   33 x 38 cm
Artist's Collection

THE TWO FRIENDS,   C.1976,   Drawing with pastel,   43 x 38 cm
Artist's Collection

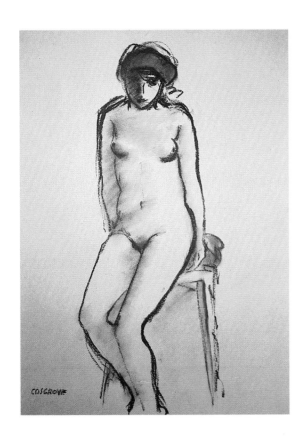

NUDE SITTING,   1978,
Pastel,   43 x 32 cm
Private Collection

BACK VIEW OF A NUDE,   1978,
Pastel,   43 x 35 cm
Private Collection

NUDE LEANING, 1978,
Pastel, 38 x 43 cm
Private Collection

NUDE LYING, 1979,
Pastel, 38 x 46 cm
Private Collection

WINTER SOLITUDE,   1978,   Oil,   51 x 61 cm
Private Collection

SUMMER LANDSCAPE,   1978,   Oil,   61 x 51 cm
Private Collection

92

THE GREEN APPLE, 1978, Oil, 30,5 x 40,5 cm
Private Collection

WINTER HARMONY, 1979, Oil on canvas, 41 x 51 cm
Galerie l'Art français Collection

JANUARY SONG, 1980, Oil, 41 x 51 cm
Galerie l'Art français Collection

THE WHITE CLOUD,   1980,   Oil,   41 x 51 cm
Artist's Collection

96

HARMONY IN GREEN, 1980, Oil, 60,5 x 70 cm
Private Collection

HARMONY IN BEIGE, 1980, Oil, 51 x 40,5 cm
Galerie l'Art français Collection

MARGUERITE B., 1980, Oil, 51 x 41 cm
Private Collection

THE BLUE RIVER, 1980, Oil, 70 x 80 cm
Private Collection

100

CHRONOLOGY

Stanley M. Cosgrove was born at Montreal on December 23, 1911.

1929 Enrolled in Montreal School of Fine Arts.

1936 Took drawing course with Edwin Holgate, at the Montreal Association School. Spent four months in the Gaspé.

1937 Painted with Maurice Raymond a mural for the Collège de Saint-Laurent. Spent his vacation in the Charlevoix region. Would return there in 1938 and 1939.

1938 Collaborated in Holgate's mural painting for the Canadian pavilion at the International Exposition at New York.

1939 Obtained a grant from the provincial government. Exhibited at the Quebec School of Fine Arts and participated in the first exhibition of the Contemporary Art Society. Left for New York with his wife.

1940 Went to Mexico at the end of January. Enrolled in San Carlos Academy in April. Stayed at Cuernavaca. Represented in the exhibition of the Anciens de l'École des Beaux-Arts de Montréal.

1941 Participated in the Exposition des Indépendants at Quebec and Montreal.

1942 Collaborated in the production of a fresco by José Clemente Orozco.

1943 Exhibited at Bibliothèque Benjamin Franklin in Mexico City. Returned to Montreal in October.

1944 Exhibited at Montreal Museum of Fine Arts. Taught decorative composition at the Montreal School of Fine Arts.

1945 Exhibited at Dominion Gallery. Taught painting at School of Fine Arts.

1948 Taught fresco at School of Fine Arts.

1949 Participated in *Quatre peintres du Québec* exhibition at Quebec Museum and at National Gallery.

1951 Became associate member of Royal Academy of the Arts of Canada.

1952 Exhibited at Dominion Gallery.

1953 Obtained a grant from the federal government. With Goodridge Roberts, visited museums in France and Spain. Painted at Côte d'Azur.

1955 Participated in the First Canadian Biennale of Painting.

1958 Left teaching and henceforth devoted himself to painting.

1961 Exhibited at the Montreal Museum of Fine Arts and at the Centre des Jeunesses Musicales at Mount Orford.

1963 Became a member of the Royal Academy of the Arts of Canada.

1969 Exhibited at the Verdun Cultural Centre.

1970 Exhibited at Klinkhoff Gallery.

1971 Exhibited at Margo Fisher-Richer Gallery in Sainte-Adèle-en-Haut.

1976 Exhibited at Kastel Gallery.

1979 Presented a retrospective in the entrance hall of Salle Wilfrid-Pelletier (Flammarion Exhibitions).

1980 Exhibited at Galerie L'Art Français.

BIBLIOGRAPHY

Books

ADAMSON, Jeremy, *The Hart House Collection of Canadian Paintings* (Toronto, University of Toronto Press, 1969).

BUCHANAN, Donald W., *The Growth of Canadian Painting* (London and Toronto, Collins, 1950).

DUVAL, Paul, *Four Decades: The Canadian Group of Painters and their Contemporaries, 1930-1970* (Toronto and Vancouver, Clark, Irwin, 1972).

GAGNON, Maurice, *Peinture moderne* (Montreal, Éd. Bernard Valiquette, 1940).

HUBBARD, Robert H., *An Anthology of Canadian Art* (Toronto, Oxford University Press, 1960); *National Gallery of Canada Catalogue*, Vol. 3); *The Development of Canadian Art* (Ottawa, The Queen's Printer, 1963).

MACDONALD, Colin S., *A Dictionary of Canadian Arts* (Ottawa, Canadian Paperbacks Publ., 1967).

McINNES, Graham, *Canadian Art* (Toronto, MacMillan, 1939, 2nd ed., 1950).

REID, Dennis, *A Concise History of Canadian Painting* (Toronto, Oxford University Press, 1973).

ROBERT, Guy, *L'Art au Québec depuis 1940* (Montreal, Les Éditions La Presse, 1973); *La Peinture au Québec depuis ses origines* (Sainte-Adèle, Iconia, 1978).

Articles from Magazines

AYRE, Robert, *Stanley Cosgrove*, in *Canadian Art*, Vol. II, No. 2 (December 1944); *From Coast to Coast — Stanley Cosgrove*. Ibid., Vol. VI, No. 4 (Summer 1949); *Conversation with Stanley Cosgrove about Orozco*, Ibid., Vol. VII, No. 2 (December 1949).

BOULANGER, Rolland, *Stanley Cosgrove*, in *Art et Pensée*, Vol. I, No. 1; *S. Cosgrove, A.R.C.A.*, Ibid., Vol. 2. No. 12).

DUMAS, Paul, *Stanley Cosgrove, peintre et dessinateur*, in *L'Information Médicale et Paramédicale*, Vol. XXI, No. 10 (April 1, 1969).

GAGNON, François-Marc, *Cosgrove et la littérature d'art officielle*, in *Vie des Arts*, Vol. XV, No. 60.

GASCON, André, *Qui est Stanley Cosgrove?*, in *Le Collectionneur*, Vol. I, No. 2.

OSTIGUY, Jean-René, *Réponse à l'article de François-Marc Gagnon*, in *Vie des Arts*, Vol. XV, No. 61.

PFEIFFER, Dorothy, *Cosgrove Exhibition*, in *The Montreal Gazette*, April 1, 1961.

ROBERT, Guy, *La Génération 1950-1960*, in *Vie des Arts*, Vol. XI, No. 44.

PRINTED BY
THÉRIEN FRÈRES (1960) LTÉE
IN OCTOBER 1980.

COLOUR SEPARATIONS BY
ADVANCED COLOUR SEPARATION OF CANADA.

PRINTED ON RENAISSANCE PAPER
ROLLAND PAPER COMPANY LTD